Illustrations by Romain Simon
Text by Lucy Kincaid

BRIMAX BOOKS   CAMBRIDGE   ENGLAND

Who is that peeping from Mother Kangaroo's pouch?
It is Kango, the baby kangaroo.
He climbed into Mother Kangaroo's pouch, which is
just like a pocket, on the day he was born, and he
has stayed there ever since. He was very tiny indeed
then, but he has grown and grown, and soon he will be
big enough to leave the pouch and hop about on his own.

lorikeet

pigmy phalanger

6

7

red kangaroo

He has already met
his kangaroo cousins.
Soon he will meet
some of the other animals
who live in Australia.

8

When Kango
left the pouch for
the very first time
he was surprised to
find his back legs
were very long,
and very bouncy.
Hop! Hop! Hop!
It was like being on a spring! Hop,
hop, hop, he went. Hop! Hop! Hop!
Here, there and everywhere.

Mother Kangaroo is
proud of her baby.
He has soft fur
and bright eyes.
He has long ears
and a strong tail.
He has springy legs
and big feet.
He can hop.
He is everything
a kangaroo should be.

KOALA

Mother Koala
is proud
of her baby too.
She is showing him which leaves
are safe to eat. Her baby
used to ride in a pouch too.
Now he rides on her back.

10

She sees the dingo watching Kango.
Kango sees it too and gets back
into his mother's pouch.
His mother can hop away from danger
faster than he can.

DINGO

11

EMU

LYRE-BIRD

The lyrebird does not fly very often.
He would rather run along the ground.

12

"Do not tread on my
tail," squawked the
lyrebird, when Kango
got too close.
"You should not trail
it along the ground,"
said Kango, and went
to get himself a
drink.

13

What a fright he had.
There was a
duck-billed platypus
swimming about in the water
looking for worms.

A duck-billed platypus
in her nest

DUCK-BILLED PLATYPUS

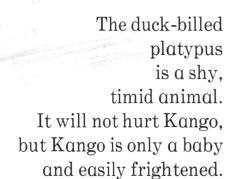

The duck-billed
platypus
is a shy,
timid animal.
It will not hurt Kango,
but Kango is only a baby
and easily frightened.

A duck-billed platypus
is a strange, mixed up,
kind of animal.
It has a bill like a duck,
a tail like a beaver,
webbed feet, and fur.
It makes a nest in
a burrow.
It lays eggs,
and feeds its young on milk.
It is one of the strangest
of all animals.

WOMBAT

Kango had another fright
early next morning. He almost bumped into a fat, tubby
wombat. The wombat had been out looking for herbs to eat and
was on his way home to his burrow. He was tired
and it was easy to see he was not feeling friendly.

16

Neither was the
cassowary bird.
He was pushing
his way through
the undergrowth with
his horny head.
He saw Kango looking
and told him to
go away.

17

Kango lay down in the sun with the other kangaroos for a
while. He felt safe with them. He knew they would not
tell him to go away. He knew too that they would warn
him of any danger, so he closed his eyes and slept for a
while.

18

19

A CUSCUS SITTING
IN A TREE

When he got older,
and less timid,
Kango often went
exploring on his own.
He made friends
with the slow
and sleepy cuscus.
He watched the anteater
eat ants.
He discovered that the
thorny devil was not
as fierce as he looked.

A BANDED ANTEATER
EATING ANTS

A THORNY DEVIL
LOOKING THORNY

helmeted honeyeater

hopping mouse

"I can hop just like you,"
boasted the hopping-mouse.
"You cannot hop as far as
I can," said Kango.

21

Leadbeaters Cockatoo

Great Black Cockatoo

budgerigar

Greater Sulphur-crested
Cockatoo

The noisy
cockatoos
were very cheeky.
"Can you do this?"
they called one day,
and they made
the feathers on the
tops of their heads
stand up,
like feathery fans.

"No!
And I
cannot fly
like the
sugar gliders
either," said Kango.
"Sugar gliders do not fly,"
squawked the cockatoos.
"You must have wings
before you can fly.
The sugar gliders
have special folds of skin
which they stretch out
and use like parachutes.
They glide.
They do not fly."

flying phalangers
(Sugar Gliders) —
sub species

The frilled lizard
opened his mouth and
spread out his frill.
He was trying
to look fierce.

frilled lizard

rat-kangaroo

He did not frighten
the little rat-kangaroo
who was scurrying about
pulling up clumps of grass
with its tail.
"Why are you doing that?"
asked Kango.
"I have a nest to make,"
said the rat-kangaroo.

24

KOOKABURRA

The kookaburra
sat on a branch
and laughed at them all.
He laughs all the time.
He cannot sing any other way.

EGRETS

26

The three white egrets
were too busy squawking
to one another to take any
notice of Kango.
Kango could hear the sheep
baa-ing, so he went to
see them instead.

27

There were sheep everywhere. Hundreds and hundreds of them, all nibbling at the grass. Kango hoped they would leave some for the kangaroos. They did. They left all the tough, dry clumps. The kangaroos did not mind that. Kango wanted to play with the tiny lamb, but its mother called it away. Kango's mother called him to come and play with the other kangaroos.

29

They were boxing. Kangaroos like boxing. They use their big strong tails to stop themselves falling over. When they are really angry they kick with their big hind feet. Today they are playing so no one will get hurt.

When they had finished boxing
they went for a long hop together.
Hop! Hop! Hop!

Everyone goes
to the waterhole
for a long, cool drink.
Kango is waiting to see
if the spiny echidna
will poke out his tongue.
It is long and thin
and very sticky.
He catches ants with it.

BROLGA

black swan

33

Kango's cousins, the rock-wallabies, are being chased by a
dingo. Dingoes are wild dogs,
and can be very dangerous.
Kango found a place to hide
and kept very still so that
the dingo would not chase him.
The little honey mouse is
looking for a hiding place too.
Kango is afraid of the wild dog.
The honey mouse is afraid of
the wild cat.

stern native cat

honey mouse

35

The danger has passed and Kango is digging a hole in the dry dusty ground. He is almost hidden when he lays down in it, but he is not hiding. It gets very hot in the middle of the day, and to lie in a shallow hole, with just head and front legs resting on the edge, is the easiest way to keep cool. All the kangaroos do it.

Kango,
his mother,
and all the other
kangaroos,
rest
at mid-day
when it is hot,
and search for food
in the evening
when it is cool.
The kangaroos
go searching
for food together.
There is safety
in numbers.
If there should be
a dingo,
or any other hunter
prowling about,
one of the kangaroos
is sure to see him,
and they they can ALL
hop away.

37

The satin bowerbird
decorates his bower
with feathers and shells.

38

SATIN BOWERBIRD

Great Grey Bowerbird

Every bowerbird has his
own special way of
decorating his bower.

Kango
is puzzled.
The female bowerbird
likes the bower
the male has built for her,
but she will not
lay her eggs in it.
She will go away
and make a nest for them
somewhere else.

Newton's Bowerbird 39

When Kango grew up
he had a family
of his own.
The baby peeping
from its mother's
pouch is his baby too.
The baby has a lot
to learn, but one day,
he will be as strong,
and as wise,
as Kango himself.

40

FOR THOSE
WHO WOULD LIKE TO
KNOW MORE

There are over fifty different species of kangaroo. The two biggest are the Red Kangaroo, and the Great Grey Kangaroo. Some of them are as big as a man. A wallaby is a kangaroo too. Some kangaroos are the size of a rabbit. Kangaroos have very short front legs, which they use rather like hands, and very long, and very strong, back legs. A big kangaroo can cover 5 to 11 yards in one jump. They always jump forwards, never upwards as that is less tiring. They use their tails to help them keep their balance.

RED KANGAROO

WALLABY

Kangaroos are very good swimmers and will not hesitate to enter the water if they are being chased.

The aborigines, who are the
original people of Australia,
have made up many stories about
the strange animals who share
their country with them.
One tells why the kangaroo always
drags his tail behind him.
One rainy day, according to the
story, the kangaroo and the wombat
quarrelled because the wombat would
not let the kangaroo warm himself
by a fire which the wombat had made.
The kangaroo got angry and attacked
the wombat with a piece of rock.
One day, the wombat had his revenge.
He delivered a blow to the base of
the kangaroo's tail, and from that
day onwards the kangaroo could not
lift his tail and had to drag it
behind him.

43

When the explorer James Cook was in Australia in 1770 he asked an aborigine the name of the bounding animal. The aborigine answered "Can-go-rou" which meant he did not understand. The aborigine did not understand the question. James Cook did not understand the answer. He thought "Can-go-rou" was the name of the animal. The aborigine name for the kangaroo is really "Walarou".

The Red Kangaroo, which grows as tall as a man, is about an inch long at birth. When a kangaroo is born it crawls up its mother's tummy and into her pouch, where it attaches itself to a nipple from which it can get milk. It will stay in her pouch for about six months. When it is six months old it will poke its head out of the pouch and look around for the first time. At eight months it will be ready to leave the pouch and go on short forays on its own, though it will still return to the safety of the pouch for a long time yet.

CUSCUS
The cuscus is a very slow moving animal about the size of a domestic cat. It has a round face and thick woolly fur. Its tail can grasp branches and it spends most of its time in the trees. The cuscus is nocturnal which means it sleeps during the day and wakes at night.

WOMBAT
Wombats have short legs and squat, tubby bodies. They are nocturnal and spend their days in burrows which they dig deep into the soil with their short, powerful claws.
Their pouches face backwards and they have only one baby at a time.

KOALA
Koalas spend almost all their time in the trees, feeding on eucalyptus leaves. They move about mostly at night. They carry their babies in pouches for three months, and then carry them on their backs. The koala's pouch opens backwards too. Some people think that the wombat and the koala may have had a common ancestor.

KOOKABURRA
The kookaburra is a member of the kingfisher family. It is sometimes called the Laughing Jackass, because of its cry, which is like human laughter. It is extremely good at catching snakes.

CASSOWARY
The cassowary is a very large bird and can grow to a height of five feet. It has a large bony helmet, called a casque, on its head which enables it to push through the undergrowth in the dense forests where it prefers to live. It can run at thirty miles an hour and is a strong swimmer.